4.99

Very Selected
Mimi Khalvati

smith|doorstop

Published 2017 by
Smith|Doorstop Books
The Poetry Business
Bank Street Arts
32-40 Bank Street
Sheffield S1 2DS

ISBN 978-1-910367-89-6

Designed and typeset by Tim Morris
Printed by Biddles Books

Acknowledgements
Grateful acknowledgements are due to the editors of the following
publications in which these poems, or earlier versions, have appeared:
The Weather Wheel (Carcanet Press 2014)
Earthshine (Smith|Doorstop Books 2013)
Child: New and Selected Poems 1991-2011 (Carcanet Press 2011)

Smith|Doorstop Books are a member of Inpress:
www.inpressbooks.co.uk.
Distributed by NBN International, Airport Business Centre, 10
Thornbury Road, Plymouth, PL6 7PP

The Poetry Business gratefully acknowledges the support
of Arts Council England.

Supported by
**ARTS COUNCIL
ENGLAND**

Contents

for Aamer Hussein

The Robin and the Eggcup

A robin flew into my room today,
into the sun of it, the wood, the plants.

A robin flew into my sleep today,
once for mischief, twice for very good luck.

A robin flew into my soul today,
queried it, rose and flumped against its glass.

So I opened it and the cold came in,
I levered it wide and the bird flew out.

Not for the first time. I let it out too,
my son said, out of the kitchen window.

No! When? Earlier, when you were asleep.
It broke an eggcup. Eggcup! What eggcup?

Not one of those nice blue and white eggcups.
Yes, he said joyfully, I swept it up.

Sonnet for my Daughter

'Come close', the flower says and we come close,
close enough to lift, cup and smell the rose,
breathe in a perfume deep enough to find
language for it but, words having grown unkind,

think back instead to a time before we knew
what we know now. When every word was true
and roses smelt divine. What went wrong?
Long before the breath of a cradle song.

Some lives fall, some flower. And some are granted
birthrights – a verandah, a sunken quadrant
of old rose trees, a fountain dry as ground
but still a fountain, in sense if not in sound.

Like a rose she slept in the morning sun.
Each vein a small blue river, each eyelash shone.

from *Entries on Light*

Scales are evenly
  weighed, inside
outside. Light is
  evenly poised
– blur to the gold
  glare to the blue –
it's twilight.
  In two minds.

Who can read by
  a lamp, focus
land's outline?
  But blue soon
sinks and gold
  rises. Who
can stay the balance
  if light can't?

Rubaiyat

for Telajune

Beyond the view of crossroads ringed with breath
her bed appears, the old-rose covers death
has smoothed and stilled; her fingers lie inert,
her nail file lies beside her in its sheath.

The morning's work over, her final chore
was 'breaking up the sugar' just before
siesta, sitting crosslegged on the carpet,
her slippers lying neatly by the door.

The image of her room behind the pane,
though lost as the winding road shifts its plane,
returns on every straight, like signatures
we trace on glass, forget and find again.

I have inherited her tools: her anvil,
her axe, her old scrolled mat, but not her skill;
and who would choose to chip at sugar loaves
when sugar cubes are boxed beside the till?

The scent of lilacs from the road reminds me
of my own garden: a neighbouring tree
grows near the fence. At night its clusters loom
like lantern moons, pearly-white, unearthly.

I don't mind that the lilac's roots aren't mine.
Its boughs are, and its blooms. It curves its spine
towards my soil and litters it with dying
stars: deadheads I gather up like jasmine.

My grandmother would rise and take my arm,
then sifting through the petals in her palm
would place in mind the whitest of them all:
Salaam, dokhtaré-mahé-man, salaam!

'Salaam, my daughter-lovely-as-the-moon!'
Would that the world could see me, Telajune,
through your eyes! Or that I could see a world
that takes such care to tend what fades so soon.

Nostalgia

'It's a night for nostalgia', he said.
I felt I was missing something, some
echo of nights we must have shared
in separate alleyways, far-off home

rain drew him back to, or clouds,
or the particular light behind rain.
I was nostalgic for words, last words
of a poem I would read on the train.

There was a power cut today. I lit
three candles, ate lamb and read
by candlelight. The beauty of it
was too lonely so I went to bed.

It rained then. In the daylight dark.
I lay there till I heard a click
and voices. When the lights came back
it was like a conjuring trick –

there they were, the animated creatures
of my life I had thought inanimate
objects. And I was the one conjured
out of their dream of a dark planet.

Villanelle

No one is there for you. Don't call, don't cry.
No one is in. No flurry in the air.
Outside your room are floors and doors and sky.

Clocks speeded, slowed, not for you to question why,
tick on. Trust them. Be good, behave. Don't stare.
No one is there for you. Don't call, don't cry.

Cries have their echoes, echoes only fly
back to their pillows, flocking back from where
outside your room are floors and doors and sky.

Imagine daylight. Daylight doesn't lie.
Fool with your shadows. Tell you nothing's there,
no one is there for you, don't call, don't cry.

But daylight doesn't last. Today's came by
to teach you the dimensions of despair.
Outside your room are floors and doors and sky.

Learn, when in turn they turn to you, to sigh
and say: You're right, I know, life isn't fair.
No one is there for you. Don't call, don't cry.
Outside your room are floors and doors and sky.

The Chine

To be back on the island is to be
cast adrift but always facing the same
mother who stays ashore, is always there
despite the mist. My balcony's a crib.
Through its bars the waves rush in. Not a ship,
not a gull, and the sky in its slow revolve
winding the Isle of Wight with a giant key.

We are spinning backwards in a slow spin;
we are in a time warp, a gap, a yawn,
a chine that cleaves the mind in two, a line
on the land's belly. Shanklin. Rhylstone Gardens
where an old man rolls tobacco, as sparing
with the strands as the years have been with him.
Luccombe with its own chine, barely a stream.

Every childhood has its chine, upper world
and lower. Time itself seems vertical
and its name too implies both bank and stream.
To be back on the island is to walk
in both worlds at the same time, looking down
on talus, horsehair fern notched through the Ice Age,
Stone Age, Bronze Age and still here at our heels;

looking up like an elf, ears cocked to silence,
from a zigzag of silver and silt. A chine
is a form of urgency to reach the sea.
As coastlines have eroded, chines, like orphans
stranded in a high place without their slope
of history, have had to take a short cut,
make deep cuts into the soft clay of cliffs.

Every path brings us back to the beginning.
Shanklin Chine is closed for the winter, both ends
barred with notices. But the mind is not.
Or memory. And time is spinning backwards
with the mainland out of sight and the great plain
where herds roamed the floor of the English Channel
and were drowned by it flush again with valleys.

I look down on them, my own that were fed
by chines, from the long esplanade of light
on Keats Green and seem to remember walking
with my mother here, running my hand on railings.
The beautiful inn on the corner's a wreck
and there, at the bend, where the light's so bright
and people walking down the steep incline

pause at the top before walking down, black
against the blaze before their torsos sink,
something vanishes, there, where the path drops
and a young boy comes running down the hill.
Never, O God, to be afraid of love
is inscribed on a new bench where I sit,
facing the headland with its crown in mist.

Song

I have landed
as if on the wing
of a small plane.

It is a song I have
landed on that barely
feels my weight.

Sky is thick with wishes.
Regrets fall down
like rain.

Visit me.
I am always in
even when the place

looks empty,
even though the locks
are changed.

Vine-leaves

Even the vine-leaves shot with sun
have shadow leaves
pressed close on them.

Even the vine is hanging
ones that seem like twos:
a top leaf
on a shadow leaf, its corner slipped,
like invoices in duplicate.

If I stood to look from the other side
with the light behind me,
would I still not see
how the top leaf shot with sun
might be the one that fails to fit
its duplicate

instead of
– standing where I do – seeing
how it is the shadow leaf that fails to fit
and failing

makes the one leaf seem like two
and being two, more beautiful?

On Lines from Paul Gauguin

How do you see this tree? Is it really green?
Use green then, the most beautiful green on your palette.
And the gold of their bodies God made to be seen?
Make love to that gold and make it a habit.

Use green then, the most beautiful green on your palette
to shadow the world always chained to your feet.
Make love to that gold and make it a habit
to leave love eternally incomplete.

To shadow the world always chained to your feet,
don't be afraid of your most brilliant blues.
To leave love eternally incomplete,
nothing shines more than the love you will lose.

Don't be afraid of your most brilliant blues.
At night phosphorescences bloom like flowers.
Nothing shines more than the love you will lose –
these are lovers' bouquets with miraculous powers.

At night phosphorescences bloom like flowers,
like spirits of the dead in a Maori sky.
These are lovers' bouquets with miraculous powers
where all the colours of the spectrum die.

Like spirits of the dead in a Maori sky
with one eye on lust, one on disease
where all the colours of the spectrum die,
paint, blind Paul, your flowers and trees.

With one eye on lust, one on disease
and the gold of their bodies God made to be seen,
paint, blind Paul, your flowers and trees.
How do you see this tree? Is it really green?

On a Line from Foroogh Farrokhzad

It had rained that day. It had primed a world
with gold, pure gold, wheatfield, stubble and hill.
It had limned the hills as a painter would,
an amateur painter, but the hills were real.

It had painted a village lemon and straw,
all shadow and angles, cockerel, goats and sheep.
It had scattered their noises, bleats and blahs,
raising a cloud, a white dog chasing a jeep.

It had travelled through amber, ochre, dust
and dust the premise of everything gold,
dust the promise of green. Green there was
but in the face of a sun no leaf could shield.

It had rained that day. It was previous,
previous as wind to seed. O wild seed,
as these words proved: 'The wind will carry us'
– *bad mara khohad bord* – and it did.

The Middle Tone

Seldom do we Andalusians notice the 'middle tone'.
An Andalusian either shouts at the stars or
kisses the red dust of the road. The middle tone
does not exist for him; he sleeps right through it.
                                    Federico García Lorca

Just so I spend my life asleep.
Stars, if there are, might shine above
and dust, dust that I've always loved,
is now dirt at most I lightly sweep.

But *cantaor*, I too exist.
My middle tone of dung and nectar,
flower and carrion, is a star
that fell, dust I too once kissed.

Ghazal: To Hold Me

I want to be held. I want somebody near
                             to hold me
when the axe falls, time is called, strangers appear
                             to hold me.

I want all that has been denied me. And more.
Much more than God in some lonely stratosphere
                             to hold me.

I want hand and eye, sweet roving things, and land
for grazing, praising, and the last pioneer
                             to hold me.

I want my ship to come in, crossing the bar,
before my back's so bowed even children fear
                             to hold me.

I want to die being held, hearing my name
thrown, thrown like a rope from a very old pier
                             to hold me.

I want to catch the last echoes, reel them in
like a curing-song in the creel of my ear
                             to hold me.

I want Rodolfo to sing, flooding the gods,
Ah! Mimi! as if I were her and he, here,
                             to hold me.

Ghazal: The Candles of the Chestnut Trees

I pictured them in the dark at night –
                    the candles of the chestnut trees.
They throw no shadow, cast no light –
                    the candles of the chestnut trees.

How many there are and each the same!
same shape and colour, angle, height –
                    the candles of the chestnut trees.

I saw how distance matters more
than nearness, clearness, to see upright
                    the candles of the chestnut trees.

Inspired by *Christ the apple tree*,
I looked for a figure to recite
                    the candles of the chestnut trees.

Lacking faith, I could do no more
than find a refrain to underwrite
                    the candles of the chestnut trees.

As May drew on, the more I saw,
the more they lost that first delight –
                    the candles of the chestnut trees.

I've searched for sameness all my life
but Mimi, nothing's the same despite
                    the candles of the chestnut trees.

Ghazal: It's Heartache

When you wake to jitters every day, it's heartache.
Ignore it, explore it, either way, it's heartache.

Youth's a map you can never refold,
from Yokohama to Hudson Bay, it's heartache.

Follow the piper, lost on the road,
whistle the tune that led him astray: it's heartache.

Stop at the roadside, name each flower,
the loveliness that will always stay: it's heartache.

Why do nightingales sing in the dark?
Ask the *radif*, it will only say 'it's heartache'.

Let *khalvati*, 'a quiet retreat',
close my ghazal and heal as it may its heartache.

Ghazal

after Hafez

However large earth's garden, mine's enough.
One rose and the shade of a vine's enough.

I don't want more wealth, I don't need more dross.
The grape has its bloom and it shines enough.

What can paradise offer us beggars
and fools? What ecstasy, when wine's enough?

Look at the stream as it winds out of sight.
One glance, one glimpse of a chine's enough.

Like the sun in bazaars, streaming in shafts,
any slant on the grand design's enough.

When you're here, my love, what more could I want?
Just mentioning love in a line's enough.

Heaven can wait. When we're under one roof,
no heaven however divine's enough.

I've no grounds for complaint. As Hafez says,
isn't a ghazal that he signs enough?

The Poet's House

The poet's house gestures towards a roof
and a chimney aslant the lemon grove
raised on the first of the bancales which climb
the mountainside towards a daylight moon.
It's like Waller's dark cottage of the soul,
dark inside but facing the rising sun
blind-eyed, its rusty ironwork balcony
with room enough for an old poet to stand,
early morning, sipping coffee, hoping,
hoping today for a visit from the muse.

No smoke from the chimney, no floor for a bed,
but something cosy as a cottage loaf
the way it nests: a square with a sense of rondure.
Does it hear the quietness of the morning
or is it, being centuries old, stone deaf?
A poet's house that was never built for song,
not for talk or companionship, for wine
or laughter. And its balcony too small
to sit there reading as the sun moves over.
Set at the foot of a slope, commands no vista.

Negatives, absences, withdrawals, withholdings,
under its red-tiled roof, hold conference.
For the soul is nothing if not negative –
look how its furniture has been abstracted,
it is all shell, shell, shell, the seed of a dwelling,
husk of an old migration. We long to possess it.
We dream of bright conversions, enough to make it
habitable: a floor, a stair, a shower;
a garden but no fence – the goats, the dogs,
would be welcome; a riot of tumbling flowers ...

I've left the door ajar, dragged vines in, greening
at their tips, it's so cool and quiet in here,
tiles underfoot covered in leaves, stalks, dirt.
Don't worry, nobody will ever come.
Even the animals, strewing droppings
along the path, know to keep away.
There's nowhere to move to, only the eye
can travel, seeing nothing but ruin, naming
nothing but ruin and the ear that listens,
through the door, for unfamiliar birds.

A Tree of Heaven, *Ailanthus altissima*,
grows near the house, its canopy bowed down
with clusters of samaras turning pink.
Sun longs to enter. Making little forays
across the grass, hanging little flags
of light along the trees. Shadows are misty
now and the face of 'Casa Fenollar'
watchful as if to call the shadows in
from where they hang precipitously by handholds
down the ravine or in the depths of branches.

But it does not call. It trusts to the campo
till, in time, of their own accord the shadows
thicken at the door and the fingers of sun
let go, sliding off the guttering.
Vast the vistas are but the casa looks
only to its own patch for it's enough
to be so wakeful and so solid. Backlit,
the Tree of Heaven flutters, edged with gold,
but why talk of heaven? Right here on earth,
Trees of Heaven grow everywhere like weeds.

Under The Vine

Yes, I should be living under the vine,
dapple at my feet and the bare dry dust

singing of drought, of heat. Look at the pile
of rubble round the roots, curled dried leaves,

mound of ant homes I can't see. Look at
the flower fallen in the dirt, flake yellow,

listen to the wasps, the bees. And the vine
above me, the vine that smells of nothing,

yields nothing but the music of its name,
the memory of some long-forgotten terrace.

Yes, under a flock of swallows that repeat
– because we have to believe it – the end,

the end, nearly the end of a summer
so long it knows neither month nor week.

Yes, I should keep my happiness hidden,
under the vine, from those who envy it.

The Waves

Every day the world is beloved by me, the seagull eager
for its perch. I woke this morning to a darkened room,

my soul stabled at the gate. We grow older, quieter,
hearing degrees of movement, distance, and the dead

would listen if they could to the voices of the living
as bedrock listens to the ocean. I listen to the waves,

trying to make them go one, two, one, two, to hear
what Virginia Woolf heard. But she heard it in memory,

darling memory that delineates. One, two, one, two,
and all the variable intervals in between surrendering

to 'the very integer' Alice Oswald rhymed with water,
creating a thumbhole through which to see the world.

Light fluctuates and my soul fluctuates like a jellyfish
underwater. My hand throws animal shadows on paper

and there, outlined, is a single goat, black and white,
standing on top of the mountain, like a tiny church.

Kusa-Hibari

It was June and every barnacled brick of the seawall
was drying out as we were. Had it been October,

had I been Hearn, I too would have kept a grass lark,
a Kusa-Hibari. Why? Not only because he sings,

not only because he is also called Autumn Wind,
Morning Bell, Little Bell of the Bamboo Grove,

or because he's worth more than his weight in gold,
being half the size of a barley grain, or even because

his antennae, longer than his body, are so very fine
they can only be seen when held against the light

as they will be held since to find him, you must turn
his cage round and round to discover his whereabouts,

but because, as his guardian tells me, his tiny song,
song of love and longing, 'is unconsciously retrospective:

he cries to the dust of the past – he calls to the silence
and the gods for the return of time' is why I'd want him.

What it was

It was the pool and the blue umbrellas,
blue awning. It was the blue and white

lifesize chess set on the terrace, wall of jasmine.
It was the persimmon and palm side by side

like two wise prophets and the view that dipped
then rose, the swallows that turned the valley.

It was the machinery of the old olive press,
the silences and the voices in them calling.

It was the water talking. It was the woman
reading with her head propped, wearing glasses,

the logpile under the overhanging staircase,
mist and the mountains we took for granted.

It was the blue humped hose and living wasps
swimming on the surface. It was the chimneys.

It was sleep. It was not having a mother,
neither father nor mother to comfort me.

Plaza de los Remedios

It's the childlike geometry of the square –
the octagonal bandstand in the centre, the ring

of café tables and chairs around it, the outer ring
of bifurcating trunks, their packed suitcases of leaves,

benches, balconies, windows that ask to be counted –
that calls to mind set squares, rulers, compasses

and a head bent over a see-through protractor,
an angle of time arrested in the impalpable air.

The scene is as mild as a nativity and beyond this
simple geometry, immense, immeasurable mountains,

a stormy Atlantic you can hear at night, snoring
like a sleeping leviathan. I would like a small life.

I would like a son who takes both my hands in his
and, walking backwards, inches me towards the end

of a cobbled street where a door opens and a daughter,
taking my hands from his, helps me over the doorstep.

The Swarm

Snow was literally swarming round the streetlamp like gnats.
The closer they came, the larger they grew, snow gnats, snow bees,

and in my snood, smoking in the snow, I watched them.
Everyone else was behind the door, I could hear their noise

which made the snow, the swarm, more silent. More welcome.
I could have watched for hours and seen nothing more than specks

against the light interrupting light and away from it, flying blind
but carrying light, specks becoming atoms. They flew too fast

to become snow itself, flying in a random panic, looming close
but disappearing, like flakes on the tongue, at the point of recognition.

They died as they landed, riding on their own melting as poems do
and in the morning there was nothing to be seen of them.

Instead, a streak of lemon, lemon honey, rimmed the sky
but the cloud lid never lifted, the weekend promised a blizzard.

I could have watched for hours and seen nothing more than I do now,
an image, a metaphor, but not the blind imperative that drove them.

The Soul Travels on Horseback

and the road is beset with obstacles and thorns.
But let it take its time for I have hours and hours to wait

here, snowbound in Lisbon, glad of this sunlit café
outside Departures, for an evening flight to Heathrow.

Being my soul's steed, I should like to know its name
and breed – a Marwari of India, Barb of North Africa,

the Akhal-Teke of Western Asia or a Turkoman,
now extinct? Is it the burnt chestnut colour of the ant,

grey as a Bedouin wind, the four winds that made it?
O Drinker of the Wind, I travel by air, sea, land

and wherever I am, there you are behind my back
pounding the cloud streets, trailing banners of cirrus

or as Platero once did, from fear or chill, hoofing a stream,
breaking the moon into a swarm of clear, crystal roses.

No, no matter your thirst, ride swiftly, mare, stallion,
mother, father, for without you I feel forever homesick.

Notes:

Page 19 – The Middle Tone
Federico García Lorca epigraph from *Deep Song and Other Prose*, ed. and tr.
Christopher Maurer (Marion Boyars, 1991).

Page 20 – Ghazal: To Hold Me
Rodolfo: Mimi's poet-lover in Giacomo Puccini's *La Bohème*.

Page 23 – Ghazal: It's Heartache
Radif: the refrain which follows the monorhyme in the ghazal.

Page 28 – Kusa-Hibari
The poem draws on and quotes from the essay of the same title by Lafcadio
Hearn, published in *Kotto* (New York: Macmillan, 1910).

Page 32 – The Soul Travels on Horseback
The poem draws on Juan Ramón Jiménez, *Platero and I*, translated by
Salvador Ortiz-Carboneres (Coventry: Dangaroo Press, 1990).

30 years
of smith|doorstop poets

Moniza Alvi, David Annwn, Simon Armitage, Jane Aspinall, Ann Atkinson, David Attwooll, Anne-Marie Austin, Sally Baker, Mike Barlow, Kate Bass, Paul Batchelor, Suzanne Batty, Zeina Hashem Beck, Chris Beckett, Peter Bennet, Catherine Benson, Gerard Benson, Paul Bentley, Sujata Bhatt, David Borrott, Nina Boyd, Maxwell Boyle, Sue Boyle, Carol Brierly, Susan Bright, Carole Bromley, Sue Butler, Peter Carpenter, James Caruth, Liz Cashdan, Dennis Casling, Julia Casterton, Claire Chapman, Debjani Chatterjee, Linda Chase, Geraldine Clarkson, Stephanie Conn, Stanley Cook, Bob Cooper, Jennifer Copley, Julia Copus, Rosaleen Croghan, Tim Cumming, Paula Cunningham, Simon Currie, Duncan Curry, Ann Dancy, Emma Danes, Peter Daniels, Peter Daniels Luczinski, Joyce Darke, Jonathan Davidson, Kwame Dawes, Owen Davis, Julia Deakin, Nichola Deane, Steve Dearden, Patricia Debney, Mike DiPlacido, Maura Dooley, Tim Dooley, Jane Draycott, Basil du Toit, Christy Ducker, Carol Ann Duffy, Sue Dymoke, Stephen Duncan, Suzannah Evans, Michael Farley, Rebecca Farmer, Nell Farrell, Catherine Fisher, Janet Fisher, Anna Fissler, Andrew Forster, Katherine Frost, Sam Gardiner, Adele Gèras, Sally Goldsmith, Yvonne Green, David Grubb, Harry Guest, Robert Hamberger, David Harmer, Sophie Hannah, John Harvey, Jo Haslam, Geoff Hattersley, Jeanette Hattersley, Selima Hill, John Hilton, Andrea Holland, Holly Hopkins, Sian Hughes, Keith Jafrate, Lesley Jefferies, Chris Jones, Mimi Khalvati, John Killick, Jenny King, Mary King, Stephen Knight, Judith Lal, John Lancaster, Peter Lane, Michael Laskey, Kim Lasky, Brenda Lealman, Tim Liardet, Katherine Lightfoot, Semyon Izrailevich Lipkin, John Lyons, Maitreyabandhu, Paul Matthews, Eleanor Maxted, John McAuliffe, Michael McCarthy, Rachel McCarthy, Patrick McGuinness, Kath McKay, Paul McLoughlin, Hugh McMillan, Ian McMillan, Allison McVety, Julie Mellor, Hilary Menos, Paul Mills, Hubert Moore, Kim Moore, David Morley, Sarah Morris, Blake Morrison, Paul Munden, Daljit Nagra, Dorothy Nimmo, Stephanie Norgate, Christopher North, Carita Nystrom, Sean O'Brien, Padraig O'Morain, Mark Pajak, Nigel Pantling, Alan Payne, Pascale Petit, Stuart Pickford, Ann Pilling, Jim Pollard, Wayne Price, Simon Rae, Irene Rawnsley, Ed Reiss, Neil Roberts, Marlynn Rosario, Padraig Rooney, Jane Routh, Peter Sansom, Tom Sastry, Michael Schmidt, Myra Schneider, Rosie Shepperd, Lemn Sissay, Felicity Skelton, Catherine Smith, Elspeth Smith, Joan Jobe Smith, Cherry Smytb, Martin Stannard, Pauline Stainer, Paul Stephenson, Mandy Sutter, Matthew Sweeney, Diana Syder, David Tait, Pam Thompson, Dennis Travis, Susan Utting, Stephen Waling, Martin Wiley, Tony Williams, Ben Wilkinson, Andrew Wilson, David Wilson, River Wolton, Sue Wood, Anna Woodford, Cliff Yates, Luke Samuel Yates